Extraordinary English

Helen Coope

In a cave far away, lives a powerful wizard named Whimstaff. He spends his days finding the answers to ancient English problems and has parchments filled with wonderful words. In this book, Whimstaff shares his knowledge to help you to master the art of English.

Whimstaff has a goblin assistant named Pointy, who is very clever. Pointy helps Whimstaff perfect his spells and gets annoyed with the laziness of Mugly and Bugly, his fat pet frogs. They spend most of their time eating and sleeping and do as little work as possible.

Pointy also helps Whimstaff look after Miss Snufflebeam, a young dragon who is rather clumsy and often loses Whimstaff's words!

Wizard Whimstaff and his friends are very happy solving English problems. Join them on a magical quest to win the Trophy of English Wizardry!

Contents

2	Mysterious Marks	18	Scary Said and Nasty Nice
4	Vexing Verbs	20	Dastardly Dictionaries
6	Super Sequencing	22	Amazing Apostrophes
8	Spooky Speech Marks	24	Puzzling Pronouns
10	Powerful Prefixes	26	Sizzling Stories
12	Revolting Recounts	28	Apprentice Wizard Challenge 2
14	Apprentice Wizard Challenge 1	30	Answers
16	Silly Singulars and Plurals	32	Wizard's Trophy of Excellence

Mysterious Marks

I'm Wizard Whimstaff and I'm here to help you become an English whizz! A sentence can end with a full stop, a question mark, or an exclamation mark. A full stop simply tells you when a sentence ends.

I'm a magician.

A question mark is used to show when a question is being asked.

How do you make a magic spell?

An exclamation mark is used when something has expression or feeling.

It was so exciting!

Task 1 Now have a go at this exercise. Put a full stop or a question mark in the brick to finish these sentences. Hey Presto!

a Where is my bag ☐

b The spell was bubbling in the cauldron ☐

c Miss Snufflebeam is a red dragon ☐

d What do dragons eat ☐

Task 2 Choose a full stop or an exclamation mark to finish these sentences. Just do the best you can!

a Wizard Whimstaff waved his wand and cried "Abracadabra ☐ "

b Every Wednesday I go to piano lessons ☐

c Whizz, bang, pop, the potion flew through the air ☐

d It was dark and quiet when we left the house ☐

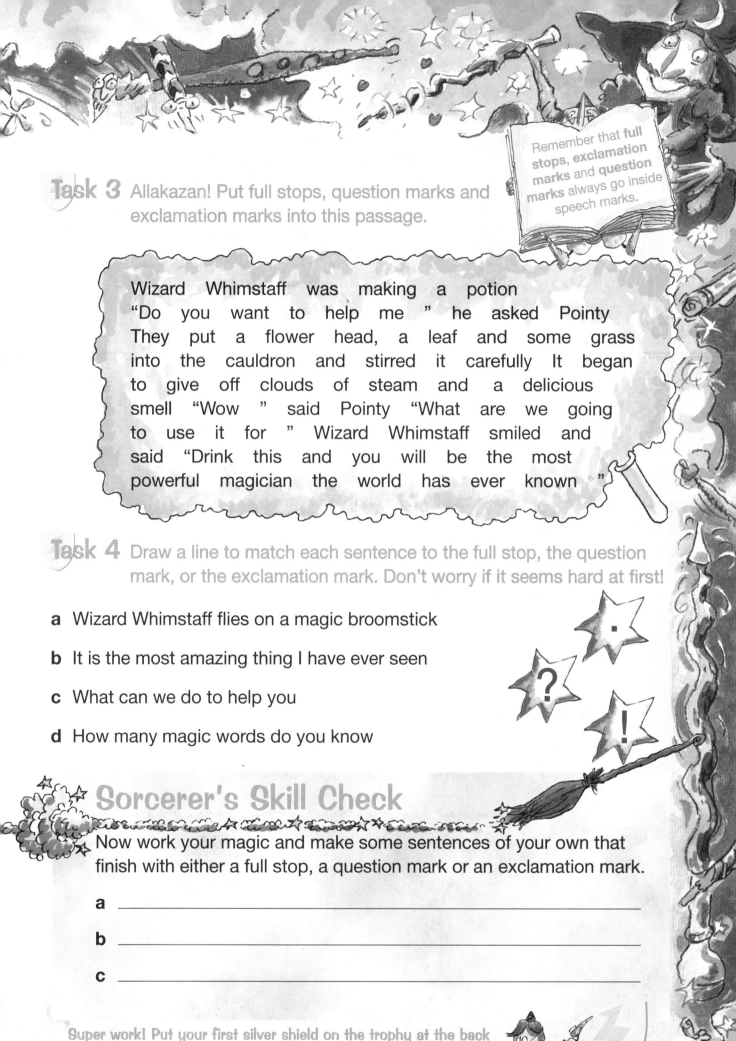

Task 3 Allakazan! Put full stops, question marks and exclamation marks into this passage.

Remember that **full stops, exclamation marks** and **question marks** always go inside speech marks.

Wizard Whimstaff was making a potion "Do you want to help me " he asked Pointy They put a flower head, a leaf and some grass into the cauldron and stirred it carefully It began to give off clouds of steam and a delicious smell "Wow " said Pointy "What are we going to use it for " Wizard Whimstaff smiled and said "Drink this and you will be the most powerful magician the world has ever known "

Task 4 Draw a line to match each sentence to the full stop, the question mark, or the exclamation mark. Don't worry if it seems hard at first!

a Wizard Whimstaff flies on a magic broomstick

b It is the most amazing thing I have ever seen

c What can we do to help you

d How many magic words do you know

Sorcerer's Skill Check

Now work your magic and make some sentences of your own that finish with either a full stop, a question mark or an exclamation mark.

a _____

b _____

c _____

Super work! Put your first silver shield on the trophy at the back of your book.

3

Vexing Verbs

I'm Pointy, Wizard Whimstaff's assistant!
A verb is an action word.

Wizard Whimstaff <u>rides</u> his broomstick.

Elves <u>dance</u> in meadows.

You can make your writing much more interesting if you try to use different verbs instead of using the same ones all the time.

You'll soon get the hang of it!

Task 1 Put circles around the verbs that almost mean the same. I have done the first one for you. Now you have a try!

a (break) (smash) drip (shatter)

d eat throw chew gobble

b climb drink ascend clamber

e watch look taste observe

c thread cook lace string

f bash hit eat thump

Task 2 Sort these words into sets of verbs that mean the same thing. It's easy when you know how!

charge cackle race sketch giggle
scribble sprint doodle chuckle

draw

run

laugh

Task 3 Put the correct verb into each sentence. Practice makes perfect!

a Pointy _____ helping Wizard Whimstaff.

b We _____ basketball at school.

c Miss Snufflebeam _____ fire.

d Wizard Whimstaff _____ spells.

e We _____ pizza with our fingers.

casts
eat
breathes
enjoys
play

Task 4 Super! Change the verbs in red for different verbs from the bottle that mean the same thing.

Wizard Whimstaff placed _____ some magic leaves in the cauldron. There was a huge puff of smoke and a whizzing noise. Pointy shrieked _____. "Don't worry," laughed _____ Wizard Whimstaff, "it's not dangerous." Miss Snufflebeam began to cry _____. She was frightened. "Quick, Pointy!" said Wizard Whimstaff. "Write _____ down the recipe before I forget it."

scribble
wail
chuckled
screamed
put

Sorcerer's Skill Check

For your final task, make some sentences of your own using these verbs on a separate piece of paper.

answer

jump

cut

cook

walk

You are clever! Give yourself a silver shield!

Super Sequencing

Hello! I'm Miss Snufflebeam and I get very confused by sequencing! I think it's about getting your ideas in the right order so that your writing makes sense when someone else reads it. We use sequencing all the time, such as in recipes and giving instructions.

Wizard Whimstaff's Vegetable Soup
Peel the vegetables with Pointy.
Put the vegetables in the cauldron.
Stir until piping hot.
Serve big portions.

Task 1 Oh no! I've muddled these instructions up. Can you number them so they are in the correct order?

How to make a card

a Finally write a message inside the card. ☐

b Sprinkle glitter over the glue. ☐

c Then spread glue inside the heart. ☐

d Next, draw a picture of a heart on the front. ☐

e Shake the card so unwanted glitter falls off. ☐

f First fold the piece of card in half. 1

Task 2 Oh dear! I've written my magic soup recipe out below in more detail. I think I've got the sequence correct, but can you write it out again for me as orders?

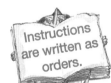

Instructions are written as orders.

Magic soup recipe details	Magic soup recipe orders
a First you boil water in the cauldron.	Boil water in the cauldron.
b You put some vegetables in the cauldron.	
c You have to sprinkle in some magic powder.	
d You must cook it slowly for 10 minutes.	
e You need to serve it when it turns bright pink.	

Task 3 Oops! I've been writing down ideas for a story plot, but I forgot to write them in sequence. Can you number the sentences in the order they should be?

a It belongs to a wizard.

b A girl finds a magic crystal.

c The wizard gives the girl a magic crystal of her own.

d A wicked old man wants the crystal.

e The wicked old man captures the girl and tries to take the crystal.

f The girl rubs the crystal and the wizard appears.

Task 4 My head hurts. On a separate piece of paper, can you write a sequence of instructions for how to make a cup of tea?

Sorcerer's Skill Check

Cabradababa! Finally, please put the missing words into this sequence of instructions.

Finally Test First Then Get Step Next

a _____ put some hot water into the bath.

b _____ add some cold water.

c _____ put in some bubble bath.

d _____ the temperature of the water.

e _____ in and enjoy your bath!

f _____ out of the bath.

g _____ pull out the plug!

Hey Presto! Give yourself another silver shield, young apprentice!

Spooky Speech Marks

We're Mugly and Bugly, the lazy frogs! **Speech marks** show us when **someone is talking.**

We are frogs.

"We are frogs," said Mugly and Bugly.

A **speech bubble** is another way of showing us that someone is talking. But that's enough talking for now, we're off to do some eating!

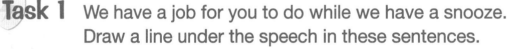

Task 1 We have a job for you to do while we have a snooze. Draw a line under the speech in these sentences.

a "Is it time to eat?" said Mugly and Bugly.

b "We are going to Grandma's house," replied Mum.

c "Abracadabra," chanted Wizard Whimstaff. "Make a magic car appear!"

d "I don't like bananas," cried the little boy. "I want an apple."

e "Can you help me?" asked Miss Snufflebeam.

Task 2 Croak! Put the speech marks in these sentences for us. We've done the first one and now we need a nap!

a "Did you know that I can breathe fire ?" said Miss Snufflebeam.

b Put on your hats and coats children , called the teacher.

c How do you make a magic potion ? asked Pointy.

d Every time we go to the funfair , said my brother , I am sick.

e Put in a toad's leg , ordered Wizard Whimstaff , then a bat's wing.

Task 3 Slurp! Rewrite what is being said in the speech bubbles as sentences, using speech marks.

a

I like chips.

_____

_____

b

I can make spells.

_____

_____

c

I love learning.

_____

_____

d

We love sleeping.

_____

_____

Sorcerer's Skill Check

Brain cell alert! Let's see what you have learned. Rewrite these sentences putting the speech marks in the correct places.

a The cauldron is bubbling, "said Wizard Whimstaff".

_____

b "Is it time to" put in the fried snake? asked Pointy.

_____

c Look at "all the smoke! said Pointy."

_____

Super! You deserve a silver shield for helping Mugly and Bugly.

Powerful Prefixes

Prefixes are magic!
They can **make new words**. They can change a word to make it mean the opposite thing.

I have used magic prefixes to change these words.

tell   <u>re</u>tell

well   <u>un</u>well

Task 1   Use your magic and have a go at this exercise. Add the prefix **un** to the word and Hey presto! See what new words you have made.

a un + happy = _unhappy_

b un + wanted = _____

c un + grateful = _____

d un + true = _____

e un + fortunate = _____

f un + fair = _____

g un + fasten = _____

h un + cover = _____

Task 2   Abracadabra! Add a prefix **dis** to each of the words in red and see how the meaning of the sentence changes.

a Wizard Whimstaff waved his wand and Pointy [ ] appeared.

b My Mum is very [ ] contented with her new job.

c Mugly and Bugly [ ] like working.

d My Dad [ ] approves of my sister's friends.

e The football team had the [ ] advantage of playing facing the sun.

Task 3 You're doing well! Now choose which prefix, **re** or **pre**, will fit these words. Don't worry if it seems hard at first.

a model — remodel

b historic —

c tell —

d call —

e locate —

f face —

g store —

h tend —

Task 4 Good work, young apprentice! Now match one of these prefixes to each word. Just do the best you can!

pre   un   re   dis

a _dis_ respect

b _____ done

c _____ form

d _____ view

e _____ trust

f _____ clear

g _____ tidy

h _____ move

Sorcerer's Skill Check

Miss Snufflebeam has messed up some of my magic words! Put a circle around each word that has an incorrect prefix.

a rearrange

b unstore

c reword

d disdo

e premature

f prepleased

Burp! That was hard work! Give yourself a silver shield and then have a snooze!

Revolting Recounts

Now I'm going to tell you about **recount** writing.

A recount tells us about an **event**. A recount is written in the order in which things happened. A recount is written in the **past tense**.

Miss Snufflebeam was practising her magic.
She made Mugly disappear!
Bugly told Wizard Whimstaff.
He magicked Mugly back again!

It's easy when you know how!

Task 1 Read this recount then answer the questions. Answer in a full sentence beginning with a capital letter and ending with a full stop. I have done the first question for you. Super!

On Sunday morning, Oscar and his family went to the station to catch the 7 o'clock train. They were going to London to spend the day at the zoo! It was the first time Oscar had been to the zoo and he was very excited. Dad carried a bag with their packed lunches in it and Oscar took his camera. The family ticket cost £12.50. The first animals they saw were the elephants. Then they went to see the penguins being fed. Mum wanted to see the bears, but they were hiding because they are very shy of people. Then they had to hurry to the station because the last train was leaving at 6 o'clock.

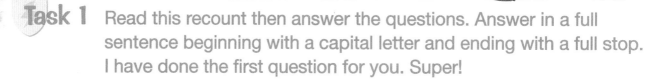

a What day did they go to the zoo? _They went to the zoo on Sunday._

b Where is the zoo? _____

c How much did the ticket cost? _____

d Who wanted to see the bears? _____

e What was in Dad's bag? _____

Task 2 Make this account a recount, by changing it to the past tense. You'll soon get the hang of it!

I go to my swimming class. I have a class at 4 o'clock. I get changed quickly, then go to the pool. My teacher is waiting for me. She tells me to swim up and down the pool four times. Then I practise diving in from the side. I get out and get dressed again. I have a hot drink before I go home.

Sorcerer's Skill Check

Look at the information below. Then wave your wand and write a recount of your trip to the cinema on a separate sheet of paper.

Joe and Ben   the cinema in town   a film called "The Haunted House"
An entrance ticket cost £3.50.   popcorn   a bus home at 5 o'clock

Hey Presto! Another task completed brilliantly. Put a silver shield on your trophy!

Apprentice Wizard Challenge 1

Challenge 1 Choose an exclamation mark or a question mark for the end of each sentence.

a How many days are there in a week

b It was the most wonderful surprise

c Wizard Whimstaff called out "Abracadabra"

d What is your favourite colour

e Will you pass me my spell book

f I have never been so scared

Challenge 2 Put a magic circle around the verb that does not mean the same as the others.

a bend   twist   swim

b brush   comb   wash

c sniff   taste   smell

d glide   cook   fly

e tie   fasten   open

f watch   stroke   pat

Challenge 3 Number the sentences in this sequence in the correct order.

a Put the mixture into a cake tin.

b First mix the butter and sugar together.

c Finally, bake in the oven for 25 minutes.

d When the eggs are beaten in, add the flour.

e Mix the eggs with the butter and sugar.

f Next beat the eggs.

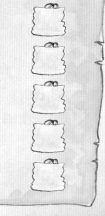

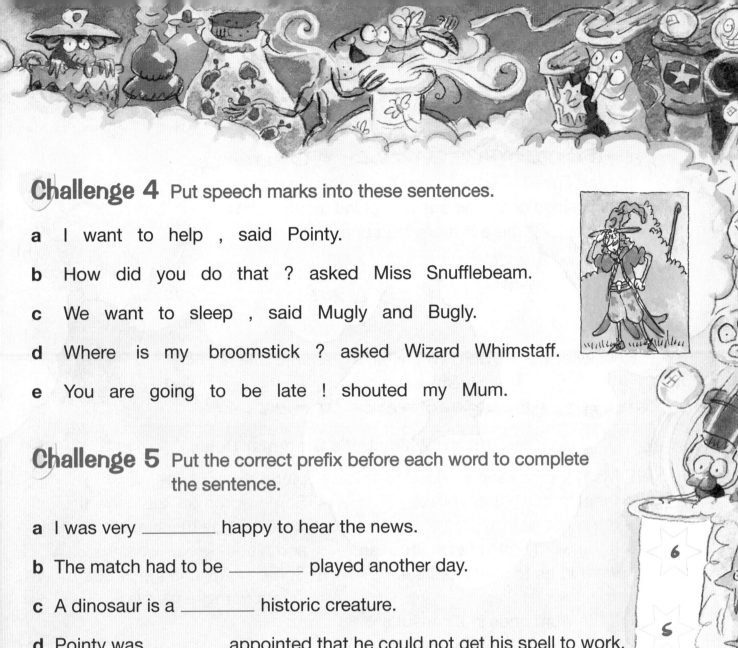

Challenge 4 Put speech marks into these sentences.

a I want to help , said Pointy.

b How did you do that ? asked Miss Snufflebeam.

c We want to sleep , said Mugly and Bugly.

d Where is my broomstick ? asked Wizard Whimstaff.

e You are going to be late ! shouted my Mum.

Challenge 5 Put the correct prefix before each word to complete the sentence.

a I was very _____ happy to hear the news.

b The match had to be _____ played another day.

c A dinosaur is a _____ historic creature.

d Pointy was _____ appointed that he could not get his spell to work.

e Miss Snufflebeam was _____ sure of what she had to do.

Challenge 6 Change the verbs in red to put these sentences into the past tense.

a We go _____ to Grandma's house yesterday.

b It is _____ her birthday.

c I take _____ her a present.

d She likes _____ it.

e We eat _____ birthday cake.

Count how many challenges you got right and put stars on the test tube
to show your score. Then have a silver shield for your trophy!

Silly Singulars and Plurals

Oh dear! I need to tell you about singulars and plurals. I think **singular** means **one** and **plural** means when there is **more than one**.

A spider.   Some spiders.

Now what were Wizard Whimstaff's grammar rules? Oh yes!

Wizard Whimstaff's Grammar Rules

1 Many words have **s** added to them to make them plural.
dog = dogs

2 If the word ends in **s**, **x**, **ch** or **sh**, we add **es** to make a plural.
watch = watches

3 If the word ends in a consonant and **y**, we add **ies** to make a plural. fairy = fairies

4 Some words do not follow this rule and stay the same in singular and plural. sheep = sheep

5 Some words change or add other letters to make plurals.
man = men
ox = oxen

Task 1 I have to match these pairs of singular and plural words. Can you help?

book	lamps
wish	babies
flame	flames
baby	wishes
lamp	books

Task 2 Oh dear! Can you help me to make these words singular?

a some stars   _a star_   **d** some lorries _____

b some foxes _____   **e** some umbrellas _____

c some owls _____   **f** some torches _____

Task 3 I'm confused! Help me to make these words plural.

Why not use a dictionary to help you find these plurals?

a a cow   some cows

b a wand

c a box

d a body

e a brush

f a spell

Task 4 Oh no! The words in red are tricky ones that don't follow the rules. Can you remember how to change them from singular to plural?

a The man _____ were working on the building.

b The sheep _____ ate all the grass.

c The woman _____ were painting the room.

d The ox _____ ploughed the field.

e The fireman _____ had to put out a huge fire.

f The child _____ wanted to learn how to cast spells.

Sorcerer's Skill Check

One more exercise and then we're finished. Put a circle around the singular form of each word and put a cross on the plural form of each word. Rabracadada!

armies		fox	cats	foxes	cat
	matches				
		dishes		broomsticks	
dish	broomstick		army		match

Slurp! You'll soon be as smart as Pointy. Another silver shield!

Scary Said and Nasty Nice

Burp! We get tired of reading stories that use the same words over and over again. Said and nice are good examples of **words used too often**! If you want to make a story interesting, you need to use as many different words as you can. Look at the difference in these two sentences.

Wizard Whimstaff cast a <u>nice</u> spell. "That's <u>nice</u>," Pointy <u>said</u>.

Wizard Whimstaff cast an <u>amazing</u> spell. "That's <u>fantastic</u>!" Pointy <u>cried</u>.

Task 1

We feel sleepy just looking at this! Put a circle around the word **said** every time it appears and a cross on the word **nice** every time it appears.

"It is a nice night," said Wizard Whimstaff. "Let's go for a fly on the broomstick."

"Nice," said Pointy. "Can we go to the haunted disco? It's nice there." "We'll see," said Wizard Whimstaff, "I thought we could go to the magic movie show. It's nice there." "Can I come too?" said Miss Snufflebeam. "I want to wear my nice new collar." "I'm sure we'll all have a nice time," said Wizard Whimstaff.

Task 2

Croak! Can you sort these words into two sets for us?

gorgeous	said	nice
replied		
lovely		
shouted		
answered		
pretty		
beautiful		
commented		

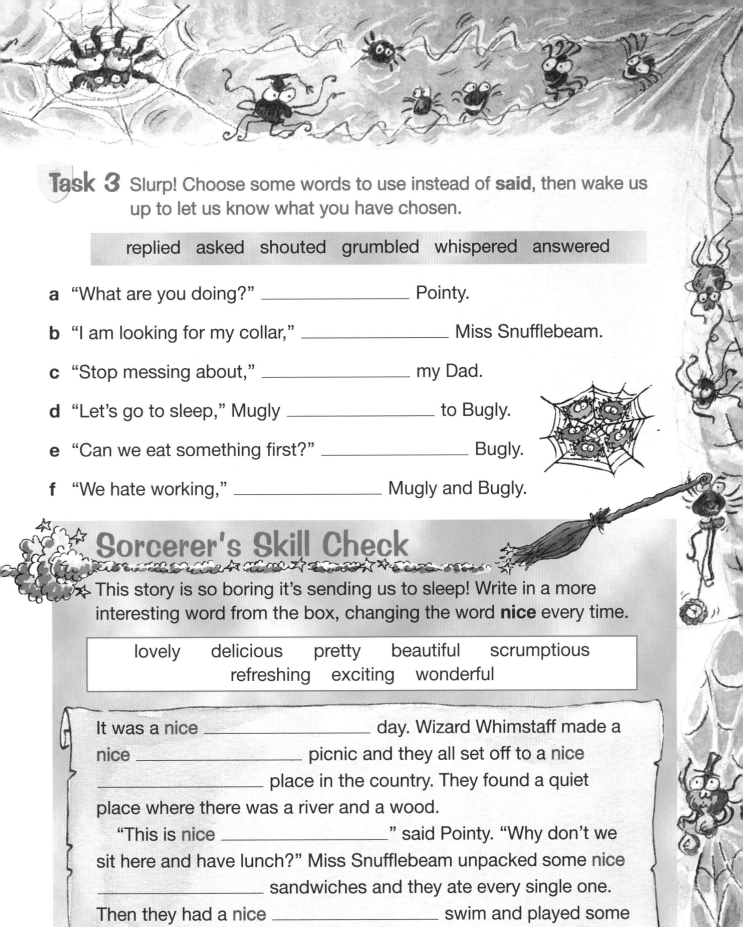

Task 3 Slurp! Choose some words to use instead of **said**, then wake us up to let us know what you have chosen.

| replied | asked | shouted | grumbled | whispered | answered |

a "What are you doing?" _____ Pointy.

b "I am looking for my collar," _____ Miss Snufflebeam.

c "Stop messing about," _____ my Dad.

d "Let's go to sleep," Mugly _____ to Bugly.

e "Can we eat something first?" _____ Bugly.

f "We hate working," _____ Mugly and Bugly.

Sorcerer's Skill Check

This story is so boring it's sending us to sleep! Write in a more interesting word from the box, changing the word **nice** every time.

| lovely | delicious | pretty | beautiful | scrumptious |
| refreshing | exciting | wonderful |

It was a nice _____ day. Wizard Whimstaff made a nice _____ picnic and they all set off to a nice _____ place in the country. They found a quiet place where there was a river and a wood.

   "This is nice _____" said Pointy. "Why don't we sit here and have lunch?" Miss Snufflebeam unpacked some nice _____ sandwiches and they ate every single one. Then they had a nice _____ swim and played some nice _____ games before going home. Everyone agreed that it had been a nice _____ day.

Fantastic work, young apprentice! You are learning fast! Award yourself a silver shield.

Dastardly Dictionaries

I have to tell you about **dictionaries**! I'll try to remember everything you need to know.

Words in a dictionary are arranged in **alphabetical order**:
<u>a</u>pple <u>d</u>og <u>f</u>ish <u>s</u>tar

When words begin with the same first letter, you look at the second letter of the words to find out which word will come first: <u>ra</u>bbit <u>re</u>d <u>ro</u>of

Dictionaries tell us what a word means. This is called a **definition**.

<u>A spell:</u> a magic poem or group of words said by a wizard.

Task 1
Can you work your magic to put these words into alphabetical order? I'm confused!

a newt frog bat spider _____ _____ _____ _____

b magic recipe spell wand _____ _____ _____ _____

c goblin dragon wizard fairy _____ _____ _____ _____

d chair bed table wardrobe _____ _____ _____ _____

e flower stem petal leaf _____ _____ _____ _____

Task 2
Help! It will be a bit harder to put these letters into alphabetical order, because they all begin with the same letter!

a cloak cauldron crow _cauldron_ _____ _cloak_ _____ crow ____

b ghost goblin gremlin _____ _____ _____

c skirt shoe sock _____ _____ _____

d wizard wand web _____ _____ _____

20

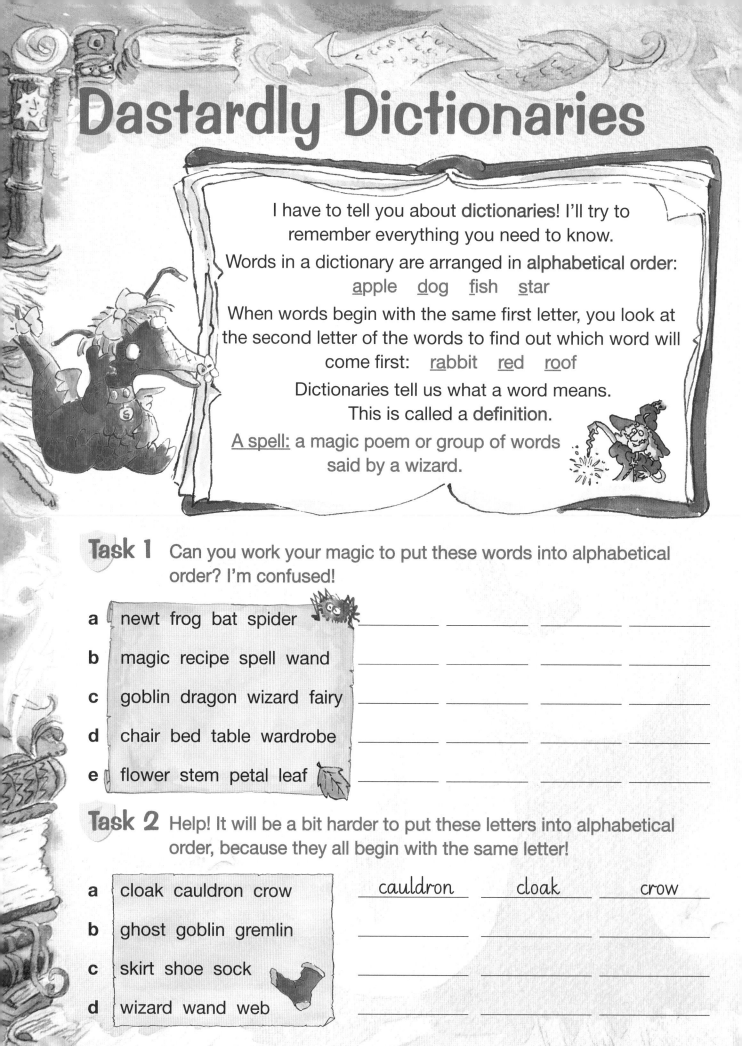

Task 3 Please wave your wand to help me match these words to their definitions.

a A pointed hat   is worn by a baby to protect clothing when eating or drinking.

b A candle   is a piece of clothing worn by a wizard.

c A bib   is what a wizard flies around on.

d A spell   is a magic poem or words said by a wizard.

e A broomstick   is made of wax and gives out light when lit.

Sorcerer's Skill Check

I have to do one final task! Can you help me put this last set of words into alphabetical order and write a definition for each word?

 toad    wizard    dragon   assistant

a _____

_____

b _____

_____

c _____

_____

d _____

_____

You have worked hard helping Miss Snufflebeam! Add a super silver shield to your trophy.

Amazing Apostrophes

Apostrophes help us with our spelling.
They make words shorter.
These are called contractions.

I am   I'm   We are   We're

They make our writing seem more like our talking.

I am eight.
I'm eight.

We are jumping.
We're jumping.

Task 1   Allakazan! Put your magic powers to the test by finding the contractions in this story. Put a circle around each one.

"We've been invited to a party," shouted Mugly and Bugly. "It says on the invitation that we're to go in fancy dress and there'll be a prize for the best costume."

"I know. It's my party," said Pointy. "You'd know that if you'd read the invitation properly. Miss Snufflebeam says she's going to dress up as a dragon."

"But she's a dragon already. She can't do that," laughed Wizard Whimstaff.

"We're going to dress up as two lazy frogs in pyjamas, ready for bed," croaked Mugly and Bugly.

"You'll stand a good chance of winning then!" smiled Pointy.

Task 2   Abracadabra! Match these words with their contractions, young apprentice!

a I am
b We are
c You are
d I will
e We would
f They have

We'd
I'll
We're
I'm
They've
You're

Task 3 Rewrite these sentences, changing the contractions into full words.

a I'm pleased with my present. _I am pleased with my present._

b We've seen a shooting star. _____

c They'll come to see you later. _____

d She's the fastest in the school. _____

e You're mixing the wrong potion! _____

Task 4 You are doing well! Can you change the words in red into their contractions?

a I would like to be a Wizard. _I'd like to be a Wizard._

b We will learn some magic spells. _____

c You are wearing a smart dress. _____

d He has cooked a spicy curry. _____

e You are getting a new bike. _____

Sorcerer's Skill Check

For your final task, fill in these missing words. Hey presto!

a You've   You have

b _____   I will

c We're

d They would

e _____   He's

f She did not

I'm sure I would have got that muddled up! You deserve a
silver shield!

Puzzling Pronouns

Me is a pronoun.
Pronouns are words that are used instead of nouns.
Look at these sentences.

Ali went to the shop with Bilal.
Ali and Bilal bought some sweets.

If we use the pronoun **they**, the sentences sound much
better when we read them.

Ali went to the shop with Bilal.
They bought some sweets.

Here are some pronouns that we use a lot:

I   me   he   him   she   her   we   us   you   they   them   it

Task 1 Match these nouns to their pronouns. I've done the
first one for you, so you'll soon get the hang of it!

a	the bat	they
b	Joe	it
c	Sara	she
d	Mum and Dad	he

Task 2 I've put a circle around the pronoun in the first
sentence. Now you have a try! Be careful because
sometimes there is more than one in each sentence!

a Patrick paid some money and ⟨he⟩ got on the bus.

b Mugly and Bugly are very lazy. They sleep all the time.

c Miss Snufflebeam loves her green collar and she wears it all the time.

d Wizard Whimstaff lets Pointy help him. He likes to teach Pointy new things.

e My aunt and uncle wanted to go to Italy but they went to France instead.

Task 3 I've written in the first missing pronoun, so now it's your turn. It's easy when you know how!

a Pointy wears triangular glasses and [*he*] loves bright clothes.

b Wizard Whimstaff and Pointy have made a new spell. [   ] are testing it.

c My brothers and I love Saturdays because [   ] watch football.

d I don't like washing up when nobody will help [   ] .

e Davina often goes to her Gran's house and [   ] always returns with a present.

f The owl tried to catch the mouse but [   ] was too slow and the mouse got away.

Sorcerer's Skill Check

Practice makes perfect! Tell me who I am talking about in each sentence.

a Mugly and Bugly love eating. **They** like to eat flies.

Who are **they**? _____Mugly and Bugly_____

b Eleanor is three. **She** can count to twenty.

Who is **she**? _____

c I help look after the school's fish. I clean **them** out every Friday.

Who are **them**? _____

d Bethany and I went to the museum and a guide showed **us** around.

Who are **us**? _____

e I got lost in a wood and no-one could find **me**.

Who is **me**? _____

Slurp! Have a silver shield while we have a nap!

Sizzling Stories

We're interrupting our snooze to tell you how to plan a good story. Stories have **characters** and **a plot**. A plot means what will happen to your characters in the story.

Stories must have:

A beginning	A middle	An end
This should grab your reader's attention.	What happens? Is there a problem to solve?	This should be strong!
The slithering noise grew closer. I hid under the bedclothes.	A dinosaur with large teeth was running towards them! It was too late to hide!	NOT And then they went to bed, BUT The Earth spun on through space, safe once again.

Task 1 Slurp! You are going to write a story while we go back to sleep. On a separate piece of paper, plan your beginning, middle and end. Write a story about one of these things:

Task 2 Croak! On a piece of paper, write a description of the setting for your story. Where would you like your story to be? A wood? A cave? The beach? The great thing about writing stories is that they can be wherever you want them to be, even another country or planet!

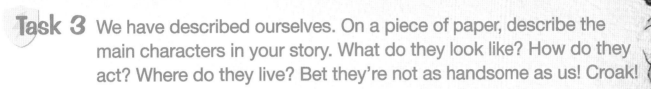

Task 3 We have described ourselves. On a piece of paper, describe the main characters in your story. What do they look like? How do they act? Where do they live? Bet they're not as handsome as us! Croak!

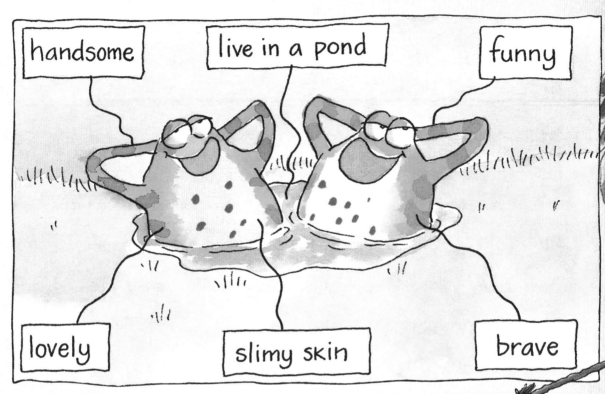

handsome

live in a pond

funny

lovely

slimy skin

brave

Sorcerer's Skill Check

Brain cell alert! Put a circle around the word we use to describe each one of these things.

		a character	a plot	a setting
a	A pirate	a character	a plot	a setting
b	A castle	a character	a plot	a setting
c	Getting caught in a storm	a character	a plot	a setting
d	A clown	a character	a plot	a setting
e	Finding buried treasure	a character	a plot	a setting
f	A museum	a character	a plot	a setting

You're a story whizz! Give yourself a silver shield.

Apprentice Wizard Challenge 2

Challenge 1   Write the singular or plural of these words.

a   a box   some _____

b   a _____   some cauldrons

c   a _____   some daisies

d   a hat   some _____

e   a sheep   some _____

f   a _____   some kisses

Challenge 2   Choose a word to use instead of **said** or **nice**.

delicious   lovely   hissed   screamed   asked   pretty

a   "Can I help?" ~~said~~ _____ Pointy.

b   It was a ~~nice~~ _____ day.

c   "Help! Help!" ~~said~~ _____ the terrified man.

d   The flowers looked so ~~nice~~ _____ blowing in the field.

e   "You look tasty," ~~said~~ _____ the snake.

f   The birthday cake tasted ~~nice~~ _____ .

Challenge 3   Put these words in alphabetical order, then write a definition
for each one.

snake   spell   scream

a _____

b _____

c _____

Challenge 4 Write the shortened form of these words using an apostrophe.

a We will ⬭

b I would ⬭

c He did not ⬭

d She was not ⬭

e They have ⬭

f You are ⬭

Challenge 5 Put a pronoun into each of these sentences.

| us | they | he | me | she |

a Miss Snufflebeam asked if _____ could help tidy the cave.

b Mugly and Bugly went for a swim before _____ had lunch.

c Pointy thinks _____ knows everything.

d Wizard Whimstaff helps _____ with our work.

e I wanted someone to go with _____ to the park.

Challenge 6 Put a circle around the word we use to describe each one of these things.

a A fairy is   a plot   a setting   a character

b A jungle is   a plot   a setting   a character

c Finding a body in the garden is   a plot   a setting   a character

d Searching for a new land is   a plot   a setting   a character

e A fireman is   a plot   a setting   a character

f A circus is   a plot   a setting   a character

6

5

4

3

2

1

Challenge Score

Count how many challenges you got right and put stars on the test tube to show your score. Then take the last silver shield for your trophy!

Answers

Pages 2–3

Task 1
a Where is my bag?
b The spell was bubbling in the cauldron.
c Miss Snufflebeam is a red dragon.
d What do dragons eat?

Task 2
a Wizard Whimstaff waved his wand and cried "Abracadabra!"
b Every Wednesday I go to piano lessons.
c Whizz, bang, pop, the potion flew through the air!
d It was dark and quiet when we left the house.

Task 3 Wizard Whimstaff was making a potion. "Do you want to help me?" he asked Pointy. They put a flower head, a leaf and some grass into the cauldron and stirred it carefully. It began to give off clouds of steam and a delicious smell. "Wow!" said Pointy. "What are we going to use it for?" Wizard Whimstaff smiled and said, "Drink this and you will be the most powerful magician the world has ever known!"

Task 4
a Wizard Whimstaff flies on a magic broomstick.
b It is the most amazing thing I have ever seen!
c What can we do to help you?
d How many magic words do you know?

Sorcerer's Skill Check
A variety of responses are correct.

Pages 4–5

Task 1
a break smash shatter
b climb ascend clamber
c thread lace string
d eat chew gobble
e watch look observe
f bash hit thump

Task 2 **draw:** scribble, doodle, sketch
run: sprint, race, charge
laugh: cackle, giggle, chuckle

Task 3
a enjoys   d casts
b play   e eat
c breathes

Task 4 Verbs fit in this order: put, screamed, chuckled, wail, scribble.

Sorcerer's Skill Check
A number of responses are suitable.

Pages 6–7

Task 1
1 First fold the piece of card in half.
2 Next, draw a picture of a heart on the front.
3 Then spread glue inside the heart.
4 Sprinkle glitter over the glue.
5 Shake the card so unwanted glitter falls off.
6 Finally write a message inside the card.

Task 2
a Boil water in the cauldron.
b Put some vegetables in the cauldron.
c Sprinkle in some magic powder.
d Cook it slowly for 10 minutes.
e Serve it when it turns bright pink.

Task 3
1 A girl finds a magic crystal.
2 It belongs to a wizard.
3 A wicked old man wants the crystal.
4 The wicked old man captures the girl and tries to take the crystal.
5 The girl rubs the crystal and the wizard appears.
6 The wizard gives the girl a magic crystal of her own.

Task 4 There is no set answer to this task, but information should be ordered in a logical way.

Sorcerer's Skill Check
a First   e Get
b Then or Next   f Step
c Next or Then   g Finally
d Test

Pages 8–9

Task 1
a "Is it time to eat?"
b "We are going to Grandma's house."
c "Abracadabra," "Make a magic car appear!"
d "I don't like bananas," "I want an apple."
e "Can you help me?"

Task 2
a "Did you know that I can breathe fire?" said Miss Snufflebeam.
b "Put on your hats and coats children," called the teacher.
c "How do you make a magic potion?" asked Pointy.
d "Every time we go to the funfair," said my brother, "I am sick."
e "Put in a toad's leg," ordered Wizard Whimstaff, "then a bat's wing."

Task 3
a "I like chips," said Miss Snufflebeam.
b "I can make spells," said Wizard Whimstaff.
c "I love learning," said Pointy.
d "We love sleeping," said Mugly and Bugly.

Sorcerer's Skill Check
a "The cauldron is bubbling," said Wizard Whimstaff.
b "Is it time to put in the fried snake?" asked Pointy.
c "Look at all the smoke!" said Pointy.

Pages 10–11

Task 1
a unhappy   e unfortunate
b unwanted   f unfair
c ungrateful   g unfasten
d untrue   h uncover

Task 2
a disappeared   d disapproves
b discontented   e disadvantage
c dislike

Task 3
a remodel   e relocate
b prehistoric   f preface
c retell   g restore
d recall   h pretend

Task 4
a disrespect
b undone
c reform
d preview or review
e distrust
f unclear
g untidy
h remove

Sorcerer's Skill Check
Incorrect: b unstore
d disdo   f prepleased

Pages 12–13

Task 1 The wording of the sentences may vary, but these are suggested answers.
a They went to the zoo on Sunday.
b The zoo is in London.
c The ticket cost £12.50.
d Mum wanted to see the bears.
e The packed lunches were in Dad's bag.

Task 2 I went to my swimming class. I had a class at 4 o'clock. I got changed quickly, then went to the pool. My teacher was waiting for me. She told me to swim up and down the pool four times. Then I practised diving in from the side. I got out and got dressed again. I had a hot drink before I went home.

Sorcerer's Skill Check
A number of answers are acceptable. This is a suggested model:
Joe and Ben went to the cinema in town to see a film called "The Haunted House."
An entrance ticket cost £3.50. They bought some popcorn. Afterwards they caught a bus home at 5 o'clock.

Pages 14–15

Challenge 1
a How many days are there in a week?
b It was the most wonderful surprise!
c Wizard Whimstaff called out "Abracadabra!"
d What is your favourite colour?
e Will you pass me my spell book?
f I have never been so scared!

Challenge 2
a swim   d cook
b wash   e open
c taste   f watch

Challenge 3
1 First mix the butter and sugar together.
2 Next beat the eggs.
3 Mix the eggs with the butter and sugar.
4 When the eggs are beaten in, add the flour.
5 Put the mixture into a cake tin.
6 Finally, bake in the oven for 25 minutes.

Challenge 4
 a "I want to help," said Pointy.
 b "How did you do that?" asked Miss Snufflebeam.
 c "We want to sleep," said Mugly and Bugly.
 d "Where is my broomstick?" asked Wizard Whimstaff.
 e "You are going to be late!" shouted my Mum.

Challenge 5
 a unhappy   d disappointed
 b replayed   e unsure
 c prehistoric

Challenge 6
 a went   d liked
 b was   e ate
 c took

Pages 16–17
Task 1 a book, books
        b wish, wishes
        c flame, flames
        d baby, babies
        e lamp, lamps
Task 2 a a star   d a lorry
        b a fox   e an umbrella
        c an owl   f a torch
Task 3 a some cows
        b some wands
        c some boxes
        d some bodies
        e some brushes
        f some spells
Task 4 a men   d oxen
        b sheep   e firemen
        c women   f children

Sorcerer's Skill Check
 Circles: army cat broomstick match dish fox
 Crosses: armies cats broomsticks matches dishes foxes

Pages 18–19
Task 1 "It is a nice night," said Wizard Whimstaff. "Let's go for a fly on the broomstick." "Nice," said Pointy. "Can we go to the haunted disco? It's nice there." "We'll see," said Wizard Whimstaff "I thought we could go to the magic movie show. It's nice there." "Can I come too?" said Miss Snufflebeam. "I want to wear my nice new collar." "I'm sure we'll all have a nice time," said Wizard Whimstaff.
Task 2 **said:** replied, answered, commented, shouted
        nice: pretty, gorgeous, lovely, beautiful
Task 3 a asked, shouted or whispered
        b replied or answered
        c shouted or grumbled
        d whispered
        e asked, answered or replied
        f grumbled or shouted

Sorcerer's Skill Check
 There are a number of correct versions. This is a suggested one.

 It was a lovely day. Wizard Whimstaff made a delicious picnic and they all set off to a pretty place in the country. They found a quiet place where there was a river and a wood.

"This is beautiful" said Pointy. "Why don't we sit here and have lunch?". Miss Snufflebeam unpacked some scrumptious sandwiches and they ate every single one. Then they had a refreshing swim and played some exciting games before going home. Everyone agreed that it had been a wonderful day.

Pages 20–21
Task 1 a bat frog newt spider
        b magic recipe spell wand
        c dragon fairy goblin wizard
        d bed chair table wardrobe
        e flower leaf petal stem
Task 2 a cauldron cloak crow
        b ghost goblin gremlin
        c shoe skirt sock
        d wand web wizard
Task 3 a A pointed hat is a piece of clothing worn by a wizard.
        b A candle is made of wax and gives out light when lit.
        c A bib is worn by a baby to protect clothing when eating or drinking.
        d A spell is a magic poem or words said by a wizard.
        e A broomstick is what a wizard flies around on.

Sorcerer's Skill Check
 assistant dragon toad wizard

 These are suggested definitions:
 a An assistant is someone who helps a senior worker.
 b A dragon is a magical creature who can breathe fire.
 c A toad is a small, warty animal that is happy on land or in water.
 d A wizard is someone who has magic powers.

Pages 22–23
Task 1 "We've been invited to a party," shouted Mugly and Bugly. "It says on the invitation that we're to go in fancy dress and there'll be a prize for the best costume."
 "I know. It's my party," said Pointy. "You'd know that if you'd read the invitation properly. Miss Snufflebeam says she's going to dress up as a dragon."
 "But she's a dragon already. She can't do that," laughed Wizard Whimstaff.
 "We're going to dress up as two lazy frogs in pyjamas, ready for bed," croaked Mugly and Bugly.
 "You'll stand a good chance of winning then!" smiled Pointy.
Task 2 a I am   I'm
        b We are   We're
        c You are   You're
        d I will   I'll
        e We would   We'd
        f They have   They've
Task 3 a I am pleased with my present.
        b We have seen a shooting star.
        c They will come to see you later.
        d She is the fastest in the school.
        e You are mixing the wrong potion!
Task 4 a I'd like to be a Wizard.
        b We'll learn some magic spells.
        c You're wearing a smart dress.
        d He's cooked a spicy curry.
        e You're getting a new bike.

Sorcerer's Skill Check
 a You've   You have
 b I'll   I will
 c We're   We are
 d They would   They'd
 e He is   He's
 f She did not   She didn't

Pages 24–25
Task 1 a the bat   it
        b Joe   he
        c Sara   she
        d Mum and Dad   they
Task 2 The following words should be circled:
        a he   d him, He
        b they   e they
        c her, she, it
Task 3 a he   d me
        b they   e she
        c we   f it

Sorcerer's Skill Check
 a Mugly and Bugly
 b Eleanor
 c The school's fish
 d Bethany and I
 e I (or my name)

Pages 26–27
Task 1 There is no set answer.
Task 2 There is no set answer.
Task 3 There is no set answer.

Sorcerer's skill check
 a a character   d a character
 b a setting   e a plot
 c a plot   f a setting

Pages 28–29
Challenge 1
 a some boxes   d some hats
 b a cauldron   e some sheep
 c a daisy   f a kiss
Challenge 2
 a asked   d pretty
 b lovely   e hissed
 c screamed   f delicious
Challenge 3
 scream snake spell

 There is no set answer, but the following definitions are examples of acceptable answers.
 a A scream is a loud, high pitched noise like a shout.
 b A snake is a long, thin reptile with no legs that slithers along the ground.
 c A spell is a set of magic words like a poem, said by a wizard.
Challenge 4
 a We'll   d She wasn't
 b I'd   e They've
 c He didn't   f You're
Challenge 5
 a she   d us
 b they   e me
 c he
Challenge 6
 a a character   d a plot
 b a setting   e a character
 c a plot   f a setting

Wizard's Trophy of Excellence

Mysterious Marks

Vexing Verbs

Super Sequencing

Spooky Speech Marks

Powerful Prefixes

Revolting Recounts

Silly Singulars and Plurals

Scary Said and Nasty Nice

Dastardly Dictionaries

Amazing Apostrophes

Puzzling Pronouns

Sizzling Stories

Apprentice Wizard Challenge 1

Apprentice Wizard Challenge 2

This is to state that Wizard Whimstaff awards

Apprentice _____

the Trophy of English Wizardry. Congratulations!